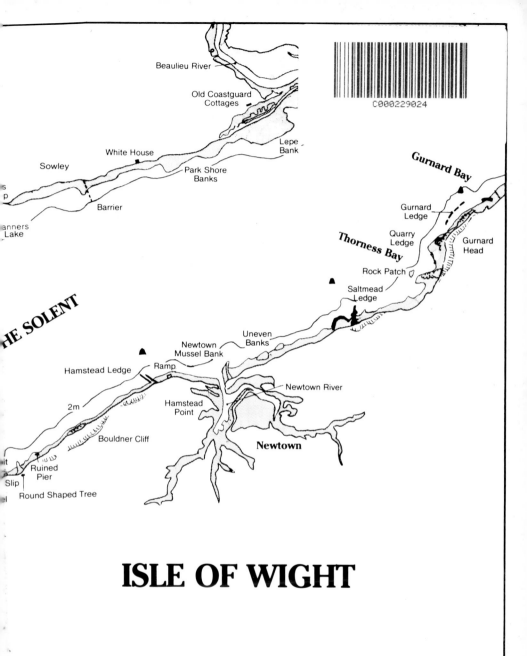

Beaulieu River

Old Coastguard
Cottages

Lepe
Bank

White House

Sowley

Park Shore
Banks

s
p

Barrier

anners
Lake

Gurnard Bay

Gurnard
Ledge

Quarry
Ledge

Gurnard
Head

Thorness Bay

Rock Patch

Saltmead
Ledge

THE SOLENT

Uneven
Banks

Newtown
Mussel Bank

Hamstead Ledge

Ramp

Newtown River

2m

Hamstead
Point

Newtown

it

Bouldner Cliff

Ruined
Pier

Slip

el

Round Shaped Tree

ISLE OF WIGHT

Nautical Miles

SOLENT HAZARDS
By PETER BRUCE

FIRST EDITION PUBLISHED MAY 1985
SECOND EDITION PUBLISHED NOVEMBER 1985
THIRD EDITION PUBLISHED OCTOBER 1987
THIRD EDITION REPRINTED SEPTEMBER 1989
THIRD EDITION REPRINTED OCTOBER 1990
FOURTH EDITION PUBLISHED NOVEMBER 1994
FOURTH EDITION REVISED JULY 1997

Other pilotage books by the same author:

Solent Tides
Wight Hazards
Inshore Along the Dorset Coast

Boldre Marine
Kestrel Cottage, Shirley Holmes, Lymington, Hampshire
SO41 8NH (01590)683106

CONTENTS

Acknowledgement

Over the nine years that Solent Hazards has been in print it has grown considerably in content, besides spawning five other similar books. Its life has been a happy and popular one, and I remain tremendously grateful to those who write in with comment or criticism. Also the pilots who fly me round the Solent, the learned people who vet the script, and finally the retailers, who cheerfully go on ordering copies of the book, sometimes thirty at a time.

Caution

While every care has been taken in compiling this book, it is regretted no responsibility can be taken by the author or publisher for inaccuracies or omissions, or for any accidents or mishaps resulting from its use.

Printed in Hong Kong by Bookbuilders

Front cover. The Needles at an exceptionally low tide. The easternmost of the Scotch boilers from the wreck of the Varvassi can be seen in the foreground.

Back Cover. A yacht stranded on The Trap with two hours still to go before low water.

Chapter 1

SOLENT HAZARDS IN GENERAL

The Solent's sheltered waters have many delights and their popularity is evident. Nevertheless there are features in the Solent which can from time to time be a source of inconvenience or worse. This book identifies these hazards, which are mainly under water, and where possible provides the local knowledge to avoid them, usually with little effort. Such information often involves using transits which, once known, are the surest method of pilotage. Some navigational knowledge is assumed and reference is often made to the local chart. It should be mentioned that this book is written for vessels of between one and two metres draught though the navigators of both deeper and shallower vessels may also find the information valuable. Detailed information regarding tidal streams will be found in the tidal stream atlas called 'Solent Tides', also published by Boldre Marine.

When in conflict with the strong tides of the Solent much advantage can usually be gained by hugging the shore. This often means venturing into shallow water which, without local knowledge, prudent mariners would take care to avoid. How close sailing vessels should go to the shore depends upon the height of the tide, the nature of the sea-bed and the strength and direction of the wind. For example, if a yacht is beating close to a gently shelving mudbank and the helmsman presses on inshore until he hears or feels the bottom rattle against his keel, then tacks immediately, the yachts's momentum may carry her through the tack. Once heeled on the offshore tack, perhaps aided by moving crew weight, the boat will be on her way again with little disadvantage. Shingle will slow a boat down much more quickly than mud, and even if the helm is put down at the moment of impact she may not get through the wind before becoming stuck fast. Grounding on rocks or sewer pipes can be a much more harrowing experience as a yacht will come to an abrupt halt with a chance of injury to crew who were standing up. Even if the yacht has not been obviously holed, the keel bolts may have been strained and the hull cracked forward of the keel. Clearly the margin of safety has to be far greater when sailing near rocks and similar solid objects, especially in a freshening wind and on a falling tide. In the case of a power vessel, expensive damage will probably be done to propellers and rudders whatever she grounds upon.

Some hazards, such as Gurnard Ledge and the Bramble Bank, are well clear of the shore and can be crossed at high water. A good navigator can quickly work out when a yacht can cross in safety, but a better one will have worked out beforehand the heights above chart datum at each hour for the expected duration of the race or passage. Computer software is available these days which provides this kind of information with great ease. It is wise to apply a safety margin, as tidal height varies with both wind direction and barometer reading. For example in the Solent a combination of a north-east wind and a high barometric pressure can lower tidal heights by 0.6m. Note that the higher the barometric pressure the lower the tide and vice versa.

A reliable echo sounder is essential, preferably with a display visible on deck and accurately marked at the point where the vessel will run aground. This can be established, for example, when the boat is dried out beside a wall for scrubbing or when she has inadvertently grounded on a flat part of the seabed. It should be remembered that the conventional echo sounder reading will vary a little with angle of heel, and the transmission will not reflect off the upper layers of soft mud.

Some experienced Solent sailors manage quite well without an echo sounder by looking ahead for abnormal ripples which may denote shallow water or rocks. For some reason in May or sometimes June, what the fishermen call 'black water' spreads up to the Solent from the Dorset coast. This water, said to be plankton rich, is clear, and for a little while one may have an underwater visibility of a metre or two. During the next four weeks the water becomes gradually more opaque as it reverts back to its normal muddy colour. Whilst the 'black water' is present it may be possible to see underwater hazards.

Should a vessel run aground and not refloat with the use of engine or crew weight, one can often obtain help from passing power craft. Racing yachts have sometimes been rescued from the mud by the wash of passing power vessels. More often power craft, with less draught than a distressed deep-keeled yacht, will offer a tow. If a horizontal pull from the bow or the stern is not successful the most effective means the assisting craft can use is to tow the grounded yacht broadside on towards deeper water by her spinnaker halliard. In the process the yacht may adopt an alarming angle of heel, but the forces involved are similar to those of a classical spinnaker broach and it is unlikely that any harm will be done. Some generous token of gratitude is usual in the event of success.

Apart from being a wonderful cruising and racing area for leisure craft, the Solent also serves the major commercial port of Southampton. Thus an above water Solent hazard, no less important than the under water hazards, is that created by commercial shipping (*Plate 1*). Restricted by lack of manoeuvrability, lack of forward vision and a draught of up to 14.9m, larger vessels are usually unable to take action to avoid a collision with smaller craft. This applies particularly during a turn, for which a ship may have to maintain a speed of up to 14 knots to achieve satisfactory control around the Bramble Bank or Calshot Spit. Such ships, being constrained by their draught, will show three all-round red lights in a vertical line by night and a cylinder by day. They may be escorted by the Southampton Harbour Master's Halmatic 42 or 44 foot patrol launches, readily recognisable by their royal blue hulls, white upperworks and broad yellow diagonal stripes showing towards their bows. They use VHF Channel 12, operate blue flashing lights when clearing a path for large commercial vessels and

Plate 1. Close enough to read QE2's name on her bow is probably too close. At the starboard yardarm she flies the triangular code pendant over flag W (for west) to indicate that she will be using the Needles Channel. Binoculars can be handy to read these signals.

their captains take a very dim view of yachtsmen mistakenly assuming right of way in the main fairway.

With the support of the Solent Area Sailing Advisory Committee and the Solent Cruising and Racing Association an 'area of concern' for yachts and small craft was established in 1993 between Black Jack and Reach Buoys off Calshot to the South Bramble and Prince Consort Buoys off Cowes. Such small vessels are now excluded from a moving exclusion area 1000m ahead and 100m on either side of a large vessel using the main channel. The previous restricted area in the Thorn Channel between Reach and Calshot Buoys and North Thorn and Bourne Gap Buoys no longer applies. Small craft, therefore, now have greater freedom of movement when shipping is not using the central Solent area, and less when large vessels are on the move. The revised system is working well and has been copied by other countries.

Even if apparently clear of an outward-bound vessel's path, it still may be important to consider which way a vessel is likely to turn. The eastern channel is the most likely, but it is worth knowing that all sizeable vessels leaving Thorn Channel are required to display a flag signal to show which channel out of the Solent they intend to take. Flag 'E' for east over the answering pendant (or code flag) means that a vessel will be rounding West Bramble buoy and heading eastwards towards the Spithead forts. Flag 'W' for west under the answering pendant means that the vessel will be making westwards for the Needles Channel.

There will normally be a UK pilot on board large vessels using the Port of Southampton. Their working frequencies on VHF are channels 12 and 14. In an emergency one should call on channel 12 and then be ready to shift to another frequency if requested.

In the same area as the large deep-draught commercial shipping there is a busy ferry service between Cowes and Southampton. The Red Funnel ferries provide a speedy service, but the quid pro quo is that small vessels have to keep a good lookout both ahead and astern and, at night, ensure that their navigation lights are showing brightly. Dangerous situations can develop rapidly at the sort of speeds the ferries use to maintain their schedules.

Red Funnel are in course of modernising their three displacement vehicle-carrying ferries. The *Cowes Castle* has already been sold, the 82m *Red Falcon* having taken her place. The *Norris Castle* is due to be replaced by *Red Osprey* in late 1994. The two new sister ships are more than twice the size of their predecessors, but will have Voith Schneider propellers for greater manoeuvrability, and hull characteristics which are intended to ensure that their wash will be no worse than the old *Castle* class. The *Netley Castle* will remain in service. She can reach 18 knots, but her normal service speed, as in the case of the *Red Falcon* and *Osprey*, is between 12 and 14 knots.

The two new catamarans, *Red Jet* I and *Red Jet* II, undertake the bulk of the work on the high speed route and need to do 22 knots to maintain a twenty minute service. There are two hydrofoils left of the original fleet, *Shearwater* V and *Shearwater* VI, now only used for back-up on the high speed route.

Other floating hazards include the many unlit racing mark buoys which are laid in the Solent in summer. These are mainly round yellow-painted steel racing marks and are shown on recent charts. The use of reflective tape has improved their visibility, but when the night is too dark to see ahead, or in thick fog without radar, one needs to plot a course to be sure of clearing them.

To describe the hazards of the Solent, an imaginary voyage will be taken with the aid of a chart, from Cowes westward up the Island coast to the Needles, across to the Shingles Bank and then eastwards along the Hampshire shore to the Spithead forts. Finally back up the Island shore again. Most of the photographs used to illustrate the main features were taken at exceptionally low spring tides and show the coastal features near chart datum. All bearings are magnetic.

Chapter 2

WEST COWES TO SALTMEAD

The Cowes area of the Solent has long been famous for first-class racing in waters where local knowledge can count heavily. Every year the general standard of competition seems to increase, bringing greater pressure on helmsmen to know precisely where they can sail and where they cannot.

COWES GREEN AND GRANTHAM ROCKS

Cowes Green, that part of the West Cowes shoreline between the Royal Yacht Squadron and Egypt Point, is one of the most popular vantage points to watch the competitors in sailing regattas such as Cowes Week. Here spectators are sometimes given a remarkable display of close quarters racing with the competing yachts only a stone's throw from the beach. Such a situation comes about when the vagaries of the Solent sea breeze cause a large part of the racing fleet to bunch at a down tide mark in the West Solent. Each boat then has to work up the shore under spinnaker towards the finishing line against the tide. On these occasions the anguish of the competitors can be appreciated by some of the rich language which wafts its way to the shore. As if this were not enough excitement, there is also a good chance that one or two competitors, hoping to minimise the effect of the contrary tide, or to clear their wind from the boats behind, will come too close to one of the many rocks that exist off Cowes Green. On a falling tide this may be where they end their day, as happened to a prince of the realm in the Cowes Week of 1992. Embarrassment such as this can readily be avoided by the observance of the simple transit described in the next paragraph.

The first hazard to note, when heading west from Number 3 buoy at Cowes harbour entrance, is a reef close in under the shore opposite the eastern end of the Royal Yacht Squadron garden, sometimes broadly known as Lion Rock (*Plate 2*). A little further again to the west, Grantham Rocks, in the shape of a hollow cone lying along the shore with its apex towards Egypt Point, extend furthest out opposite the houses built closest to the shore (*Plate 3*).   As already mentioned, it is quite easy to become stuck on Grantham Rocks, or trapped in the hollow when cheating the tide along this shore, thus it is fortunate that

Plate 2. The north-west corner of Cowes Harbour. Patches of rocks can be seen off the RYS pier and off the RYS garden, the latter being generally known as 'Lion Rock'.

there is a simple rule for the avoidance of both Lion Rock and the entire Grantham Rock ledge. The white painted structure at Egypt Point, which is all that remains of the old light, is easy to identify; and some 25m to the east there is a statue of a semi-rampant lion on a plinth. A transit between the Egypt Point light structure, while it still remains, and the lion's nose on 272° takes a yacht down a line just outside the outer limit of all these rocks (*Plate 4*).

The beach is clear of major rocks to the west of the new beach shelter with its pyramid-shaped roof, though it is wise to go outside the post marking the council slipway opposite the New Holmwood Hotel. One can safely go close in at Egypt Point itself, but one cannot do so to the west of the point.

Plate 3. Cowes Green and Grantham rocks.

Plate 4. Looking west at the transit between the old Egypt Light structure and the statue of a semi-rampart lion. The post with the green cone marks the end of a slipway.

11

GURNARD BAY

As far as navigation is concerned the salient feature of Gurnard Bay is Gurnard Ledge (*Plate 5*). This ledge is composed of clay and limestone, and appears at extreme low springs in the middle of Gurnard Bay running westwards towards Thorness Bay. When coming from the direction of Egypt Point it is easy to find the gap between the ledge and the shore on the way in, but it is not always so easy to find the gap at the west end on the way out. The ledge is not an obvious hazard; it is well out in the tideway, steep-to, and whilst the Gurnard Ledge Buoy is clear enough, it can be difficult to judge where the ledge itself is. Occasionally fish floats are laid at some point along the ledge which can be helpful in the short term, as is the yellowy colour in the water appearing down tide from the ledge, caused by the erosion of the clay. The eastern end of Gurnard Ledge is in line with the Gurnard Sailing Club flagstaff and the third window from the right of the large building on 086°, a pub called the Woodvale (*Plate 6*). This transit is particularly useful when a decision has been made to pass outside Gurnard Ledge but inside the Gurnard Ledge Buoy. No convenient transit exists for

Plate 5. Gurnard Ledge, looking south-east. Notice that the tidal stream has just started to flood inshore of the ledge and is still just ebbing offshore of it.

Plate 6. The east end of Gurnard Ledge is in line with the Gurnard Sailing Club flagpole and the right-hand front corner of the Woodvale Pub.

Plate 7. A course about 50m north of Baxters Buoy will find the deepest water between Gurnard Ledge and the Island shore.

finding the deepest water at the west end of the inshore passage, but some guidance is given by a round white dinghy racing buoy marked GSC and called Baxters, which is laid in summer off Quarry (or Baxter's) Ledge *(Plate 7)*. A course about 50m north of this buoy should give a minimum of two metres at the western gap in Gurnard Ledge, but one cannot, of course, depend on the position of the buoy. If in doubt it is best to err towards the Island shore.

Due to the infamous ledge, Cowes race officers usually avoid setting courses which take yachts into Gurnard Bay immediately after their start; but circumstances may be such that competing yachts become drawn in there later on in the race to avoid the tide. For example many of the yachts taking part in the first race of the 1981 and 1993 Admiral's Cups went aground on Gurnard Ledge. Also the yachts *Big Apple* in 1977 and *Blizzard* in 1987, with well known skippers at the helm, are known to have come to a dramatic halt on its eastern corner. More recently the Irish Team Admiral's Cup yacht *Jameson 1*, owned by King Harald of Norway and, incidentally, sailed by the same helmsman who was in *Big Apple* in 1977, sank there after going aground on the 29 July 1993. Other yachts in the race were severely damaged.

If there is not enough water over Gurnard Ledge to ignore it alto-gether, a decision has to be made as to whether to take the inshore passage inside Gurnard Ledge, or pass outside it. If working along the shore from Egypt Point, one should take into account two series of rock outcrops. The first of these includes some wreckage, reputedly of a World War II German bomber, and lurks just round the corner from Egypt Point opposite a bungalow *(Plate 8)*. The second and more prominent lies between the recently rebuilt and stockaded gas pressure reduction station - a flat-roofed building at near road level - and the houses to the south-west (*Plate 9*).

Plate 8. The reefs to the west of Egypt Point light structure. The most prominent rocks are off the bungalow just to the west of Briary Court, the large collection of buildings in the centre of the picture.

A new Gurnard sewer outfall in the form of twin 20cm pipes has been laid on the east side of Gurnard Bay, opposite the point where Princes Esplanade reaches the level of the beach. The unmarked discharge is 400 metres out from the shore and the pipes are entirely buried. The construction of this outfall replaces the two other Gurnard sewer pipes which are now storm overflow pipes. Near high water most yachts can continue along the shore round to Quarry Ledge, or Baxter's Ledge as it is known locally, with some confidence. They can cheat the tide to good effect in the knowledge that they are comfortably inside Gurnard Ledge should there be insufficient water to pass over it. Even so the inshore route should not be undertaken lightly. For example, when heading to the west, care should be taken to leave both green conical buoys marking the end of the storm overflow pipes in the bay on the port side.

14

The eastern green storm overflow buoy, marking the Woodvale out-fall, is off Gurnard Sailing Club and gives a useful reference point when approaching the rock ledges extending out from the shore to the south of Gurnard Bay. The pipe itself, of 0.3m diameter and well in on the beach, has a concrete block sticking up about a metre above the surrounding level. This is now marked by a green post with a double green triangular topmark, the two triangles being set at 90° to each other. The Gurnard Marsh storm water overflow outfall lies about 350m to the west. Its pipe diameter is 0.5m and it extends 230m out to sea. Beside it there are pedestals and a larger concrete block of a previous pipe removed in 1977. These stick up rather higher than the level of the existing pipe but the large concrete block - no one seems to quite know why the Victorians made these constructions - is now marked with a post and double triangle similar to that marking the Woodvale pipe.

To the west of the Gurnard Marsh storm water outfall the shore looks rockbound at high water. In fact the rocks along the shore give way to sand not far beneath the surface and there are no surprises until Gurnard Head itself has been reached. Thus an echo sounder will give adequate warning of shallow water if tacking along the shore.

Plate 9. Gurnard Bay, showing the inshore rocks, and storm drain pipes.

15

Plate 10.   Quarry Ledge   (or Baxters Ledge) looking south-east.
See also Plate 15.

THORNESS BAY

At the promontory between Gurnard and Thorness Bays, Quarry Ledge, or Baxter's Ledge as the locals prefer to call it, sticks out like a clenched fist 220m from the shore (*Plate 10*). It can catch those over-anxious to reach the weaker tides of Thorness Bay or those in the bay working soundings eastwards.

A clearing transit to the north is given by the Woodvale Pub in line with a prominent green-roofed beach house on 066°. Another clearing transit to the west used to be given by lining up the Rowridge TV mast with the triangular measured distance beacon, but both the Thorness red and white chequered measured distance beacons, which were erected during World War II, presumably to allow vessels to calibrate their logs without leaving the protection of the Solent, were perma-nently dismantled in the autumn of 1991 at the request of the Ministry of Defence land agency.

Apart from Quarry, or Baxter's, Ledge there are other rocks to beware of in Thorness Bay. A line of rocks stretches out from the shore towards the centre of the bay and some way to seaward of this an

16

Plate 11. Looking south-east into the eastern corner of Thorness Bay. The isolated patch of rocks in the foreground shows up clearly. Note the cables crossing the promontory and amongst them the recently laid concrete covers for the high voltage cables

Plate 12. The rock ledge at the west end of Thorness Bay, looking north-west.

isolated patch of rocks exists (*Plate 11*). Both of these hazards may be recognised by choppy water over them, fish floats and surface weed. Opposite the wooded part of the shore, there is a bank of rocks with a post in the midst of them marking the end of a sewer outfall coming out from the adjoining holiday centre (*Plate 12*). This post does, by chance, help to mark the rock ledge as well. Yet another rock ledge extends out from the shore before one arrives at Salt Mead. This lies opposite the part of the coast where a lumpy incline of bare soil and scrub leads up to trees on the skyline.

There are no high-profile rocks amongst the ledges described thus far, but nor is there a great tidal advantage once inside the line of Gurnard Head and Hamstead Point. Consequently it is as well not to try to work this shore too closely, even at high tide, when strings of seaweed from the ledges float to the surface, and can be a nuisance. Nevertheless small craft may want to take advantage of an east-going eddy which is to be found on a spring ebb tide close to the shore in both Thorness Bay and Gurnard Bay from two hours after high water Portsmouth.

Chapter 3

SALT MEAD LEDGE TO YARMOUTH PIER

SALT MEAD LEDGE

Salt Mead Ledge (*Plate 13*) can come as a surprise when approached from either direction, so an early offing may be necessary. Rather than running at right angles to the shore, the ledge leans towards Cowes. Thus when beating westwards on soundings along Thorness Bay, it is possible on the offshore tack to encounter Salt Mead Ledge with the keel. The ledge is steep on its western side, so when coming from the west avoiding action may be necessary before soundings give warning. The ledge extends submerged further out into the Solent than the photograph indicates, its extremity being often marked by fish floats and choppy water (*Plate 14*). It is worth remembering that the ledge lies opposite Burnt Wood, another plantation which comes down to the shore (*Plate 15*).

Plate 13. Salt Mead Ledge looking north. Salt Mead Ledge Buoy is in the top left-hand corner.

Plate 14. Broken water and fish-floats marking the extremity of the Salt Mead Ledge.

Plate 15. A north-easterly view from Salt Mead Ledge to Quarry Ledge.

Plate 16. Looking north-east from Newtown River entrance. The yacht on the left didn't quite make the channel.

HAMSTEAD LEDGE

Hamstead Ledge is a deeply submerged promontory, but inshore of it are two parallel rock bars of Bembridge Limestone (*Plate 17*) which are of more interest to owners of leisure craft. These extend westward at an acute angle to the shore rather further out than the ledge shown on charts. The inner ledge extends to the west of the barrier and there is only about 0.4m depth over it at chart datum. Lesser parallel bars lie further inshore and extend well to the west of the barrier.

Just to the west of Salt Mead lies a semi-circular rock pattern, and beyond this there are some uneven banks before a mussel bank running northwards from the shore about 200m short of the Newtown River entrance. It is worth mentioning that on the last three hours of a spring ebb, the tide comes out of Newtown River entrance faster than some vessels can sail or motor.

Plate 17. The ledges off Hamstead Point, looking south.

Plate 18. The remnants of the stone pier off Bouldnor, looking east.

At Hamstead Point the shore can be approached closely until opposite a large concrete ramp built at high water level at a gap in the trees. This ramp is at the site of the boom defence depot in the last war where flotation buoys were launched for the boom between Hamstead Point and Durns Point. The posts of the Hamstead Ledge barrier were removed in 1996 and those off Durns Point may be removed too.

BOULDNOR CLIFF SHORE

Between Hamstead Ledge and Yarmouth Pier the shore is uneven with occasional rocky patches and three sand spits. There are two off-lying features, a ruined stone pier and a rock called The Camel.

Five hundred metres off the west end of Bouldnor cliff, shown at a depth of 6.3m, lies the wreck of a gravel dredger, the *Margaret Smith*, which capsized on 28 June 1978 after her cargo had shifted. Inshore of her the remnants of the stone pier can be seen which was constructed in the 19th century for loading bricks made in kilns nearby. All that now remains is a square-shaped base 65m from the cliff face, on which a stone wall stands rising about 5m above the surrounding sea bed level (*Plate 18*). The wall, which is never covered at high water, runs north-south and, whilst coming as something of a surprise, this old and rather beautifully laid masonry does not extend significantly beyond what can be seen. Thus a very shallow-drafted craft can even pass safely between the ruins and the shore at high water, but beware sand spits to the east and to the west. Not far beyond the stone pier a stream, marked by reeds, can be seen on the shore. Offshore of the stream a lump of mud forms an island at low water.

Plate 19. The shoreline between Bouldnor and Hamstead Point. The remaining piece of wall of the Stone Pier shows up as a light-coloured speck against the dark seaweed-covered base. Note the sand bars on either side of the stone pier.

23

Plate 20. The Camel showing at low water spring tide. Note the abutment in the sea wall and the oak tree in line behind it.

Further on, one mile east from Yarmouth Pier, another sand spit sticks out to the east of the private slipway at Eastmore House. Until it falls over, this can usually be located by reference to a round shaped and distinctively-leaved tree growing outwards from the cliff face above the base of the spit (*Plate 19*).

Less than half a mile east of Yarmouth Pier the chart shows Wilmingham Road intersecting the coast road with a bank of 0.8m depth extending 425m offshore. The bank needs to be given a generous allowance at low water; moreover an isolated hump on it, thought to be made of concrete and known as the Camel (*Plate 20*), dries 0.4m at chart datum. This obstruction is roughly 1.5m across and protrudes about half a metre above the surrounding depth. It may be marked by an unofficial float, for example at one time by a green plastic one gallon engine oil can. The Camel is situated on a flattish rock ledge about 170m from the shore and can be found by lining up the end of Yarmouth Pier with the distant boarded up coastguard look-out tower at Hurst on a bearing of 272°, then proceeding a few metres until the eastern gable of the pink house, called Waterside, which stands at the western end of the buildings on the shore, is in line with the nearby abutment in the sea wall on a bearing of 181°. Should the abutment not be easily visible, the large oak tree in front of the house serves equally well as an alternative so long as it remains in place. One can be sure of being clear to the north of the Camel and the outlying rocks on the same plateau by keeping all of Hurst Spit fully in view to the right of Yarmouth Pier.

Four hundred metres east of Yarmouth Pier, and at a depth of about 5m, lies a 16th century protected wreck, marked by a large yellow buoy. She is now thought to be the Spanish merchant vessel *Santa Lucia* which sank in 1567 when bound for Flanders with a cargo of wool.

YARMOUTH PIER

As part of renovation work, Yarmouth Pier was made shorter by some 6.7m during the winter of 1993-1994 and the Round House moved accordingly. This has affected the transits which could be used to avoid the Camel and Black Rock.

It is a regrettable fact that, on rare occasions, fishermen on Yarmouth Pier have been known to hook passing yachtsmen, so it is wise to be on guard when sailing close to the end of the pier. As a result of these occurrences there is a notice to the effect that seafarers have a right to pass close to the Yarmouth Pierhead, and have right of way over fishing lines! Note that when the Union flag is replaced by a square red flag on the pierhead flagpole, this means that Yarmouth Harbour is full. The intention of the signal is to save vessels from having to turn round in the narrow entrance of the harbour.

Chapter 4

YARMOUTH ROAD TO WARDEN LEDGE

YARMOUTH ROAD

The principal hazard in Yarmouth Road is the rocky plateau known as Black Rock (*Plate 21*) which lies about half way between the Black Rock Buoy and the shore. It is shaped roughly like a triangle, with a 70m base running parallel with the shore, and a 20m apex, pointing south. A clearing bearing is 97° on the end of Yarmouth Pier. As an alternative to using a hand bearing compass one can devise another transit by using the end of Yarmouth Pier again and ensuring that the the end of the pier lines up on the deciduous trees behind, rather than the gently sloping conifers on the sky-line (*Plate 22*).

Inside Black Rock there is a wide and shallow inner passage, and this may be used at high water on the way to and from Yarmouth Harbour, but care should be taken to avoid lumps opposite the breakwater which dry out at low water springs. To the west of the breakwater, a transit for the inshore passage is provided by lining up the end of

Plate 21. Black Rock at low water. Note that Black Rock Buoy is well to the north of the rock itself. Also that the first of the flood can be seen in this photograph inshore of the rock.

Plate 22. Black Rock can be cleared by keeping the end of Yarmouth Pier in line with the nearer deciduous trees of Bouldnor, rather than the more distant pine trees on the skyline. This line takes a vessel well inside Black Rock Buoy.

Plate 23. A transit between the end of Victoria Pier and the lookout tower at Hurst gives the deepest water in the channel between Black Rock and the Yarmouth shore. Most craft can only use this channel at high water.

Victoria Pier with the lookout tower at Hurst Point on 272° (*Plate 23*). A plan has been under consideration to remove Black Rock Buoy, which is now maintained at the expense of the Yarmouth Harbour Commissioners, rather than Trinity House, and replace it with a lit isolated danger beacon erected on Black Rock itself. But as the present buoy and cable are in good condition no imminent action is likely. There is another plan under review to build an outer harbour for visiting craft.

Two unmarked pipes shown on the chart run out to sea from Norton. The longer one, just to the west of Black Rock, was constructed in 1980 and is mostly buried. The shorter pipe, marked 'Disused' on the chart, is sometimes partly exposed above the seabed level near to the shore.

SCONCE POINT TO WARDEN POINT

One can approach the beach closely at Sconce Point, but further west, where a useful eddy forms on the ebb, the shore shelves less steeply. There is a sprinkling of small rocks on the beach about half way between Sconce and Round Tower Point, and between Round Tower Point and Fort Albert there are spits of rock and sand (*Plate 24*). The rocks are most prominent off Round Tower Point. The outermost drying rock is on a line between the right hand side of Fort Albert and the cleft

Plate 24. A view of Round Tower Point and Fort Albert, looking south-west.

Plate 25. The prominent rocks off Round Tower Point are cleared by keeping the distant old coastguard cottages on West High Down in view to the right of Fort Albert, as shown in this photograph.

in the skyline created by the dry moat at the Needles Old Battery. All these rocks are clear inshore if a vessel is north of a transit between the square outline of the old coastguard cottages on the skyline at Tennyson Down - or, to be more exact, West High Down - and the right hand wall of Fort Albert (*Plate 25*).There is a wreck of a small tug which was bombed in World War II, lying buried in the sand between Round Tower Point and Fort Albert. Her diesel engine has toppled over, but still projects nearly a metre above the surrounding sand level.

Another spit of low profile rocks, extending north from the north jetty of Fort Albert, can catch out craft coming in from the Needles. Local fishermen call this Fort Albert Ledge and they use the line of a fence running up the hill from the corner of the breakwater on a bearing of 162° to place it. One is in deep water on this line if Tennyson's Cross is visible, and not obscured behind the right hand edge of the fort.

Charts show How Bank, How Ledge and How Reef in Colwell Bay

Plate 26. How Ledge in Colwell Bay and Warden Ledge, looking south-east. Note the patch of rocks to the east of How Ledge (above the yacht) and the isolated patch of rocks to the east of Warden Ledge disclosed by the white flecks of broken water.

to the west of Fort Albert (*Plate 26*). Viewed from the air, the submerged How Ledge can clearly be seen, marked by a number of lobster pot floats. To the north-east of the tip of How Ledge a more isolated rock can also be seen not far beneath the surface. This ties in with the submerged rock shown on the chart at the western tip of How Bank. There has been a report of another isolated submerged rock about 200m to the north-east.

Warden Ledge, which divides Colwell Bay from Totland Bay, is much like How Ledge but on a larger scale and more prominent. If passing inside Warden Ledge Buoy, floats and choppy water caused by the tidal stream should roughly indicate its whereabouts. However there is also a most useful transit between the cleft on the skyline and Hatherwood Point and on a bearing of 222° giving at least two metres over How Bank, How Ledge and Warden Ledge except, perhaps, on an unusually low tide (*Plate 27*). This becomes especially valuable when avoiding the full strength of the contrary tide by edging in towards Colwell Bay and Totland Bay.

On 4 May 1989 the maxi-yacht *Belmont* (ex-UBS), a one time Whitbread Round the World Race winner of draught about 3.5m, was carrying out sailing trials in the Needles Channel in company with another maxi-yacht called *Rothmans*. *Belmont* struck a rock off Warden ledge an hour before low water spring tide and as a result of this stranding her navigator was sacked. Careful transits, supported by photographs, were taken by Michael Wason of Totland, and from these it seems likely that *Belmont* had encountered an uncharted rock outside the five metre line. The skipper of *Belmont* was made aware of this possible defence but the navigator was not reinstated.

Plate 27. By keeping north of a line between Hatherwood Point and the cleft in the skyline on a bearing of 222°, vessels of moderate draught will be clear of all the rocks in Colwell and Totland Bays.

Chapter 5

WARDEN POINT TO THE NEEDLES

TOTLAND BAY

Once well past Warden Ledge, Totland Bay is clear of offshore rocks, but to the west of the bay there is a reef lying parallel to the shore some 100m out, which begins 750m south-west of the pier (*Plate 28*). The bigger rocks at the east end of this reef are called the Upper Penner and the Lower Penner. The iron post still shown on the chart

Plate 28. Looking east at the rocks off the cliffs between Totland Bay and Alum Bay.

Plate 29. Looking south from Hatherwood Point to the corner of Alum Bay.

some 100m to the south-east of the Penner Rocks has long since fallen over. A transit to comfortably clear the Penner rocks is given by a pair of specially painted white posts at the lower end of the flight of steps at Widdick chine. The steps are just to the west of the old lifeboat house, the isolated blue-doored building above the sea wall. To the west of the Penners there is a dense semi-circular pattern of rocks then a separate cluster. The reef is about 350m long, and beyond it the coast is rocky with a heavy scattering of hard stuff off Hatherwood Point following round into Alum Bay to just short of the chair lift (*Plate 29*).

ALUM BAY

The 'Hatherwood Rock' shown on the chart, which also used to be known by some local fishermen as Five Fingers Rock, has lost its individuality. Nonetheless there are plenty of nasty rocks on this corner. Five Fingers Rock, as charted, has 1.9m over it at datum, and therefore will seldom be a hazard to most craft. I confess that I have never managed to find it.

There is now nothing above water left to see of the original Alum Bay Pier which was built in the latter half of the nineteenth century. It started to collapse in 1927, and then was partially demolished in 1942. The outer pier post, which was leaning at a drunken angle for many years, has now fallen further over and, though perhaps not quite horizontal, is said to be well covered (*Plate 30*). Two upright submerged stumps, just 2m and 7m inshore of where the outer post used to be, still exist and, now that the outer pier post has disappeared, they are more of a hazard than they were before. A new small pier was built to the south of the old one in April 1987.

Plate 30. Looking south-east into the corner of Alum Bay. The photograph still shows the last above surface post left standing from the old pier, 60m offshore from the bottom of the track leading from the wood. Further into the bay one small vessel seems to have found herself right over the eastern Long Rock, while the yacht on the right hand side of the picture has anchored inshore of west Long Rock.

Plate 31. East Long Rock awash at low water springs. Note that the left hand extremity of the chair lift is in line with the bottom of the steps.

Apart from the old pier stumps the greatest perils of Alum Bay are the offshore rocks 200m apart rising sharply some 5m from a flat seabed.   The western one, described as the Long Rock on the chart, hardly ever shows, but the eastern rock, which runs like a peaked wall parallel to the Needles, appears at a quite ordinary low water spring tide (*Plate 31*).   The owner of the new jetty and of the Needles pleasure boat '*Wild Rose*' has placed a rust coloured 0.36m diameter round marker buoy just to the north-west of the east Long Rock. The ring on the top has been cut off to discourage visiting yachts from trying to use it as a mooring buoy. The western Long Rock is sometimes marked by a fish float. Otherwise both Long Rocks are a little difficult to place, par- ticularly the western Long Rock. It is helpful to know that if the left hand end of the Hurst fortifications is in line with the toe of Hatherwood Point one is between east and west Long Rock; a line from the right hand end of Hurst fortifications to the toe of Hatherwood Point takes one close to the east side of west long rock.   Bearings from western Long Rock are: top of chair lift pylon 068°, chimney of house in corner of cliff 103°, right hand chimney pot of the old coast guard cottages on West High Down 210° and Needles Light 253°. On this latter bearing the bot- tom right-hand corner of the central red band of the lighthouse is roughly in line with the right-hand sloping edge of the outer Needle at low water.

Inside the Long Rocks, in the very corner of Alum Bay, there is a ledge called Plattagen Rocks which never quite dries.   A Fairmile launch was beached there in the early seventies after hitting the Mid

Shingles Buoy in the night, and some parts of her, such as a propeller shaft, still remain.

Six hundred metres west of the corner of Alum Bay, about 35m from the foot of the cliff, there is an iron post sloping acutely eastwards which dries about 1m at chart datum, and is thus able to give another nasty surprise to those venturing too close to the shore (*Plate 32*). The post is believed to be the remains of a pre-war practice target and is toppling over a little more every year (*Plate 33*).

Plate 32. The iron post off the white cliffs of Alum Bay.

Plate 33. The Needles looking south at low tide. Both of the outer gaps are often 'threaded' by local craft. More details can be found in the companion volume to Solent Hazards, 'Wight Hazards', also obtainable from Boldre Marine.

THE NEEDLES

Passage around the Needles lighthouse is made perilous by the presence of a wreck which causes serious damage to any number of small vessels every year. The 3,874 ton ship *SS Varvassi* went aground in clear weather at 0700 on 5th January 1947 carrying a cargo of strong wine and oranges: a welcome event locally at the time. Her remains are positioned as shown on the chart, but her hull has almost entirely broken up leaving only pieces of her propulsion machinery intact. Of those which are a hazard, the most inshore are two squat Scotch boilers which sit on their ends like twin saucepans. The boilers are about four metres in diameter and have a height of about 2.5m. They have large holes in the end plates at the top. Nearby lie the remains of her reciprocating steam engine and shaft, then a little further out the ship's stern tube. Some hull structure lies in deeper water to the west as well as her propeller, which is cast iron and therefore not worth salvage. The most inshore boiler is 100m from the base of the lighthouse, and both of the boilers are exposed at chart datum. The engine and the stern tube have a least depth of 0.5m and 0.7m respectively in a surrounding depth of 2.8m. These dangerous remnants of the wreck lie in the line of the Needles on a NNE/SSW heading and are well wedged by rocks, so they cannot possibly move about as has been sometimes suggested (*Plate 34*).

It is difficult to judge distance off when rounding the Needles, so it is wise to give the wreck a wide berth. A safe rule of thumb, giving at least 4m depth, is to make sure the lighthouse main light is buried in the coastguard station when the Needles are in line. It is possible to venture between the wreck and the light but such a course, with the nearly sheer-sided Goose rock to the north-west of the light on the one hand and solid boilerplate on the other, cannot be recommended unless the whereabouts of these two objects are known. Minimum depth found within this passage is probably about 2.4m at chart datum. Deeper water, up to 3m at chart datum, is on the lighthouse side. A vessel approaching from Alum Bay and intending to use the inshore passage from north to south should not pass south of a line between the highest point of the middle Needle and the coastguard station until it is judged that Goose Rock has been passed (*Plate 35*). Likewise when going from south to north a vessel should not turn to the east towards Alum Bay until north of this transit.

Various schemes to deal with the dangerous parts of the wreck have been proposed but have been found too costly or impractical to

Plate 34. An overhead view of the Needles showing Goose Rock and the four dangerous hunks of wreckage further offshore. Note the tide race running between the inner boiler of the wreck and Goose Rock.

Plate 35. Goose Rock can be avoided on a course from Alum Bay by keeping the old coast-guard station on West High Down in sight when rounding the Needles between the lighthouse and the wreck.

implement. Unofficial buoys are laid from time to time and it may be that a proper wreck buoy may be laid one day. Apparently there are three bulging files at Trinity House filled with impassioned requests for some action to deal with the dangerous parts of the wreck. However it is the policy of Trinity House to only mark hazards in passages used for general navigation.

From a marine archaeologist's point of view there are two interesting protected wrecks close-in off the Needles. One of these is a 44 gun warship, *HMS Assurance*, built in 1747 at Heather Yard, Bursledon and wrecked on Goose Rock in 1753 whilst carrying home the retiring governor of Jamaica. The other is another warship, a frigate of 38 guns called *HMS Pomone*. She was built on the river Medway in 1805 and was lost in 1811 after hitting a rock off the Needles on her way into the Solent at night. Survey work, mainly involving divers from a naval club, is still active and care should be taken to avoid sub-aqua swimmers if a diving tender is seen to be operating. Some of the artefacts recovered from these wrecks can be seen at the Royal Naval museum beside *HMS Victory* at Portsmouth.

Chapter 6
THE SHINGLES TO LYMINGTON

Accidents are common at the entrance to the Needles Channel, not only because it can be particularly rough there, but also because the transition for incoming vessels between an open water situation to a close inshore situation takes place in an unusually short space of time. Conversely outgoing vessels can be caught out by an abrupt change from the sheltered waters of the Solent to short, steep, breaking seas. In unsettled weather the good seaman will have secured his vessel properly for sea, have his crew equipped with oilskins, sea boots, lifejackets, safety harnesses and seasick pills, and will be carrying a sensible amount of sail before Hurst Castle is abeam. In severe weather he will avoid the Needles Channel altogether.

THE SHINGLES

Ancient maps show rock pinnacles appearing above the surrounding level of the Shingles Bank but, if they ever did exist, they have long since gone. Nowadays there is no danger of hitting a rock on the Shingles Bank and one can even sail over the Shingles at high water on a calm day, when the eerie noise of loose shingle in motion can sometimes be heard. Nevertheless embarrassing encounters with the Shingles have occurred at the start of more than one Round the World Race, when the excitement of the occasion and proximity of many spectator craft must have confused the competitors. Even shallow-draught craft should allow a good margin for unexpected lumps which can be formed by gales or the tide (*Plate 36*). Fifty years ago the Shingles appeared more frequently at low water than they do now though remarkable gravel islands showing about two metres at high water do emerge from time to time. There is one shown on the Admiralty chart of 1921 off Elbow Buoy, one appeared during World War II, another appeared for two months in the spring of 1988 off Elbow Buoy again, and yet another off the Mid Shingles Buoy in early 1990 (*Plate 37*).

On the ebb there is a strong west-going cross tide on the north side of the channel causing craft to be set onto the Shingles Bank. Conversely the flood tide carries craft away from the bank.

In addition to the shoals, when passing over or close to the

Plate 36. Shingles banks often appear at low water spring tides, but not always in the same place.

Plate 37. Gravel islands form from time to time on the Shingles and show well above sea level at high water.

Shingles one should look out for breaking seas. Even if only the slightest swell is running, waves can appear as if from nowhere to capsize even quite sizeable vessels. According to the Needles Lighthouse keepers of yore, waves over the Shingles tend to break more on the flood tide than the ebb.   In a south-westerly gale ferocious breaking waves can extend from the Shingles across into the Needles Channel, leaving nowhere completely safe. Usually the calmest water will be found near the Bridge Buoy, though in moderate conditions some prefer to take a course half way between the Bridge Buoy and the Needles Lighthouse where three or four vicious seas may be experienced but that will be all. Alternatively one can take the North Channel which is sheltered from the full force of the swell by the Shingles Bank. Invariably the seas are calmer in the North Channel and there is the benefit of a favourable eddy when the main Solent tidal stream is ebbing. The North Channel is generally to be preferred though use of this passage demands that one has to round up towards the wind just short of a lee shore, and should anything go wrong at this juncture a vessel could soon drift onto Hurst Spit. Thus in really extreme westerly gales there is a strong case for approaching the Solent via Spithead or staying at sea until the weather moderates.

HURST POINT TO LYMINGTON

Hurst Castle was one of a series of anti-invasion coastal fortresses built by Henry VIII, using the proceeds from the suppression of the monasteries. Hurst Castle was completed in 1544, but the original structure is largely hidden from seaward by two massive casemented wing batteries which were constructed between 1861 and 1879 to deter hostile French ships from entering the Solent. The shells from the 38 ton rifled muzzle-loading guns were said to have been able to penetrate wrought iron metres thick. The dark and menacing effect of the casements is due to heavy iron shields which were an important defensive feature of the fortifications. As it happened none of the mighty nineteenth century Solent defences were ever put to the test.

King Charles I was imprisoned briefly in Hurst Castle in December 1648 prior to his trial and execution in 1649. Subsequently the castle was designated as a prison for those convicted for fostering the growth of Popery. A priest named Father Paul Atkinson suffered this fate in 1700 and was to remain in Hurst Castle for the rest of his life. Thereafter no one else, it seems, chose to foster the growth of Popery. A small community lived at Hurst at one time, enough people including the soldiers from the battery, to support three inns, the Shipwrights Arms, the New Inn and the Castle Inn.

As far as yachtsmen are concerned Hurst is also famous for its well-named Trap (*Plate 38*). This sand spit sticks 60m out into the channel opposite the first black casement of the eastern wing battery, and gives little warning on an echo sounder. Aerial photographs taken since 1983 show that The Trap, as might be expected, varies quite considerably in height and extent. At the time of writing it is more prominent than usual. When entering the Solent against an ebb tide and making use of the eddy on the west side of Hurst beach, it is advisable

Plate 38. Looking north at the tip of Hurst Point. The sand bar, aptly named The Trap, is quite evident just east of Hurst Castle itself.

to head decisively into deeper water before the circular-looking Henry VIII castle which can just be seen above the level of the wing batteries, the so-called Round Fort, is on the beam. Those who have been stuck on The Trap report that the ebb tide holds back the Channel swell, which then reappears on the flood tide with startling force. Beyond The Trap, heading east, one is in deep water again and can pass close to the south-east tip of Hurst Spit.

There is noticeable erosion of the shore line on both sides of the spit, except at the south side of the Keyhaven river mouth where, curiously, the spit is extending by three to five metres a year. In particular the whole of the western side of Hurst Beach is suffering from erosion and recently the spit has been temporarily breached in storms (*Plate 39*). This has given rise to local concern, and various attempts have been made at reinforcement. The current repair plans will cost at least £4.6 million and will entail the construction of a new groyne at the Castle end and a breakwater to enable the reinforcing shingle to be landed. Six hundred thousand pounds has already been spent upon research, planning and design so it is to be hoped that those concerned with the project will have more luck than King Canute.

After closing on the Hampshire shore, a sounding can be picked up and followed past Hurst Spit (*Plate 40*) and Pennington towards the Lymington River. Navigators of deep-draughted large yachts will notice that the seabed shelves rapidly once Hurst High Light is past the beam. An orange dinghy racing mark between Hawkers and Stivers Lakes, when laid, gives an indication of how far in a yacht can go at high water (*Plate 41*). The lone rock shown on the

Plate 39. Hurst Beach the day after it was breached in a storm.

Plate 40. Looking south-east from North Point to Hurst Point.

chart off Hawker's lake does not exist. Hawker, by the way, was a celebrated Keyhaven 19th century sportsman and the author's great-great-great grandfather! He was invalided from the army after being seriously wounded whilst serving under Wellington. Though his injuries were to trouble him for the rest of his life he spent much of his time in demonstrating how one could bring to the oven some of the great abundance of wildfowl to be found on the marshes, an extremely popular accomplishment before the days of supermarkets. He also took command in Keyhaven emergencies, such as the breaching of the sea wall, besides supervising and paying for Hawker's Lake, the useful short cut into Keyhaven named after him (*Plate 42*).

On both sides of Pennington sewer beacon, particularly to the east, the bottom is lumpy to the extent of half a metre. At low water vessels drawing more than two metres can get caught out along this shore, as shoal water extends out beyond the line of the Pennington sewer beacon

Plate 41. Looking east towards Hawkers and Stivers Lakes. Note the offshore mudflat between these two lakes.

and Jack in the Basket. In particular, there is a ridge of shingle running parallel to the shore south- east of the Pennington sewer post with less than half a metre over it at chart datum (*Fig 1*). There is another less pronounced ridge to the south-west of Jack in the Basket. Various hard objects have been reported on the seabed from time to time particularly in the area of the Pennington sewer outfall.

The marshes off Keyhaven and Lymington are retreating at the

Plate 42. A high tide view of the marshes between Hawkers and Coles Lake. Iley Lake connects Stivers and Coles Lake to Hawkers Lake, and all are navigable by dinghies at high water.

rate of 4-5 metres per year due to erosion and the die-back of spartina grasses. The spartina grass only appeared around the turn of the last century and there is no obvious reason for its decline. It may be simply due to natural evolution. Other plants such as sea purslane and sea lavender are appearing to take the place of the spartina grasses but are not likely to affect the rate of erosion. The extent of the marshes in the past can be seen on old maps but, in spite of marked diminution, there are still many channels that can provide an enjoyable pasage

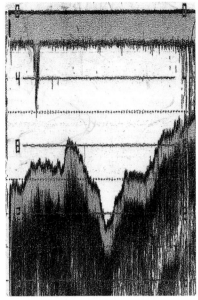

Fig.1. A south-north sounding run to the east of Pennington sewer post showing the shingle ridge. The sounding are in feet.

for dinghies at high tide. At low water, in addition to the shingle, there are odd places where a dark spongy substance can be seen on the shore between Hurst and Lymington. This comes from submerged peat beds such as may also be found at low water along the shore around Yarmouth. In addition to the peat beds, close inspection of the gravel at Pennington beach will show that some of it is common flint stone, as might be expected, and some of it is smoothly rounded wood from ancient forest which at one time commonly grew to the water's edge of the whole south coast of England. The peat beds and the forest were submerged when the sea level rose 12m between 6000 and 3000 years ago.

The 1.5m Pennington sewer pipe laid in 1980 lies in a trench and is not a hazard, though the raw outflow has nothing to commend it. An overdue treatment plant is due to be brought into use at the end of 1995.   The only part that protrudes above the sea bed is the T piece diffuser, which is 2m in height, and is located 6m inshore of the sewer beacon. The two outer sections of the old pipe were never removed, so it is said, and still lie to the north of the sewer post but in deep enough water to present little, if any, risk to passing craft.

The sea wall between Lymington and Keyhaven has recently been renovated at great expense (*Plate 43*). The previous one was reputed to have been built by French prisoners of war in the 19th century. Behind the wall there is still evidence of Lymington's salt pans which, for six hundred years, were the principal source of the nation's salt. The back end of the recess in the old wall opposite Oxey Lake, called Oxey Dock, can still be seen. This was where barges took the ground to disembark Kentish coal used in the dehydration process before reloading with salt for distribution and sale elsewhere. Mounds can also be seen inside the sea wall on which windmills were built to pump the salt water from the salt pans to the boiling houses.

When the present Pennington sewer outfall was constructed, the sewer pipe of Oxey, half a mile to the east, was removed except for its supporting concrete pedestals which, in some places, appear above the seabed. Since the removal of the pipe, Oxey Lake and Narrow Mark channels leading to the Lymington River through Crooked Lake, or to the Yacht Haven, have become useful to small craft at high water (*Plate 44*). As a matter of interest rather than concern, during World War II a German bomb is said to have landed in the mud on the south side of Crooked Lake without exploding. In addition, not far away, a

Plate 43. Middle Island, Oxey Lake and Norrey Lake at high water, looking towards Lymington.

Plate 44. Shell Island in the foreground, and the Oxey Lake, Norrey Lake and Crooked Lake channels which can enable shallow-draughted boats to reach the Lymington Yacht Haven at high water without use of the Lymington River fairway.

Gannet aircraft crash-landed on Shell Island in the 1950s. It was winched to a lighter in the river which accounts for the straight grooves in the marsh which can still be seen from the upper passenger deck of the Lymington-Yarmouth ferry. On the subject of these ferries, one should mention that though, at low water, they take up almost all the channel in the Lymington River their Voith Schneider propellers make them highly manoeuvrable even when stationary. Unlike shipping and ferries in the area between Cowes and the Hamble, they are seldom a problem to smaller craft in the open Solent.

Chapter 7
LYMINGTON TO CALSHOT
LYMINGTON TO THORNS BEACH

In November 1977 the Lymington Spit Buoy was removed but the spit itself still exists.   Part of this is a bank extending about 100m south and 400m south-east from the Royal Lymington Yacht Club starting platform, and it is possible to go aground here at low water when approaching the Royal Lymington Yacht Club line to the south of the platform.   Between the starting platform and Tanners lake the mud banks vary in height by at least half a metre and in random manner confounding even the locals, but at half tide or more one can make a useful hitch into Pylewell Lake, and work close to the bank at high

Plate 45. Looking north-west towards Lymington. Very small craft can enter Tanners Lake at the bottom right hand corner of the picture, take the cutting into Freshwater Lake and thence to Pylewell Lake, arriving off the Bag of Halfpence post in the Lymington River.

Plate 46. A shallow channel, where bird life prospers, running between Tanners Lake and Pitts Deep Lake.

Plate 47. The shoreline gradient between Pitts Deep and the Sowley Boom is quite gentle.

water. Pylewell creek dries out, but at high water it provides a useful and lovely short cut for small craft, water ski boats permitting. Another creek, called Freshwater Lake, can take one east from the Pylewell inlet, coming out into the Solent opposite Tanner's Lane via a narrow canal (*Plate 45*). Eastwards from Tanners Lake provides another attractive inland waterway, emerging at Pitts Deep (*Plate 46*). Off the saltings at Sowley (*Plate 47*) the sand comes further out and changes appreciably from year to year. The metal posts of the wartime barrier off Durns Point, marked as an obstruction on the chart and often called the Sowley Boom, are increasingly falling over with age. Inspection at low tide suggests that all these fallen posts lie flat on the seabed, though there is always a possibility that one will be left at an angle just below the surface. It is, therefore, wiser to go round them rather than through the gaps. There are plans to remove the boom in due course.

The chart shows an area between the posts off Durns Point and Hamstead Point where anchoring and trawling is prohibited. This is another legacy from the second world war when a steel wire boom was positioned between the two barriers as a defence against hostile submarines. No doubt obstructions such as sinkers and wire cable were left on the seabed when the boom was removed at the end of the war which would account for the prohibition. Local trawler fishermen say that the only obstruction which is known to be in existence is a concrete

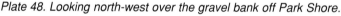

Plate 48. Looking north-west over the gravel bank off Park Shore.

Plate 49. Looking north-east over the Park Shore banks. Note the Beaulieu mudflats beyond and the inlet opposite Lord Montague's beach house.

block in deep water opposite the northerly barrier, so it is possible that not much remains on the seabed. An anchor, on the other hand, is more likely to snag buried cables than a trawl; therefore perhaps one should continue to heed the restriction.

Beyond the barrier, the bottom is moderately shelving up to the treacherous Park Shore shingle banks (*Plate 48*). The first of these is south of the white house at Thorns Beach. There follows a deceptive indentation followed by abrupt shoals which often catch the unwary. On the west side of this bank there lies SSW/NNE a 20m long metal pipe of 0.3m diameter, sometimes marked with a plastic float, and which dries at low water springs. A fence extending 150m into the sea marks the eastern limit of the Park Shore banks, and the transit of the eastern of the two beach houses and the Fawley Power Station chimney gives a clearing line (*Plate 49*).

THE LEPE BANK

A large stretch of sand and mud, extending well out into the Solent and called the Lepe Bank, lies off the old coastguard cottages at Needs

Plate 50. Looking north-west to Needs Ore Point and to the causeway blocking off the Swatchway (or Bulls Run). Note that the Beaulieu Spit mudbanks in the foreground are rather lumpy.

Ore.   At high water one can pass over it, but at other times it presents a large flat obstacle.   An awkward channel in the form of a dog-leg lies between Lepe Bank and the shore, where there is about 0.5m more water than to seaward.

THE BEAULIEU SPIT

The Beaulieu spit extends from Needs Ore to the Beaulieu river entrance. The short cut at Needs Ore, known as the Swatchway or Bulls Run, was closed in 1986 to protect Gull Island against continuing erosion, which was expected to affect Exbury Marshes and the anchorage in the first reach of the river (*Plate 50*). The channel could be reopened if the closure was to prove ineffective, but, on the contrary, the erosion is said to be now much less severe. To seaward of Gull Island the bottom is quite lumpy and it is wise to give a margin of half a metre or so. Beaulieu Spit is extending eastwards and to seaward. When approaching the river entrance the deepest water will be found east of the transit.

STANSORE POINT

The banks on the east side of the Beaulieu River entrance can be

Plate 51. Looking north-east at Stansore Point and Horseshoe Spit. Only the eastern of the three original posts remains, but may soon be removed.

approached with the aid of an echo sounder. Six cables to the east of the dolphin at the Beaulieu River entrance there is a shingle bank coming out from Stansore Point known locally as Horseshoe Spit (*Plate 51*). This pronounced spit extends 580m south from the shore. The extreme southerly point is some 360m south-west from the remaining beacon which is due to be removed by the end of 1997. At high water spring tides most yachts will pass over Horseshoe Spit, but at other times it is advisable to stay well south of it. Keen racing crews may wish to use some feature ashore as a tide gauge which will indicate when their boat can cross the spit.

The eastern edge of the bank off Stansore Point runs on an approximate line between the beacon and the point. At high water springs one can approach the shore closely to the east of Stansore Point, and pass closely to or even between the two dolphins marked on the chart. However the eastern side of the shingle bank at Stansore Point can vary quite markedly, and a number of

Plate 52. Exposed steel pipeline on the east side of Horseshoe Spit.

Plate 53. An exposed steel pipe seen from sea level. These pipes may have been the cause of several heavy groundings.

heavy groundings occurred during the 1992 Cowes Week on a spit which has built up around an apparently redundant steel pipe about mid-way between the eastern-most beacon and the prominent wooden tapering oil rig-like structure on the shore (*Plate 52*). Two Sigma 38s, *Yeoman XXVIII* and *Profit*, and a Channel Handicapper called *Highlander* were amongst those which went aground whilst on a southerly course. Others in their class on the same tack but further inshore towards Horseshoe Spit managed to escape it. This spit may be the obstruction shown on the chart reported in 1988 as 'position approximate' (*Plate 53*).

Many Isle of Wight service pipes and cables run over from Stansore Point along the seabed to Egypt Point, Gurnard and Thorness Bays. Though the pipes are well buried in the sea bed inshore, they are largely exposed further offshore so the prohibited anchorage area exists for good reason. Every year anchors foul the cables. For example, in 1992 there were two incidents where the steel wire armour of a power cable was sufficiently damaged to cause the insulating oil to leak out. In one incident the damage was done by a motor cruiser's anchor which the owner did not want to lose. He requested help and in doing so revealed his identity. Later he was presented with a bill for the damage to the cable which would probably have paid for hundreds of anchors. In the other incident, which occurred in shallow water on the east side of Stansore Point, it seemed likely that a yacht's keel had caused the problem. In addition to the three 132Kv power cables of 14 cm diameter, there are also three steel gas pipes of 10mm wall thickness and 0.3m external diameter including the concrete coating. There are two water pipes and three telephone cables. Finally there appear to be other, probably redundant, pipes which appear in places on the surface of the shingle at extreme low water spring tides. These are the ones which probably caused the trouble in the 1992 Cowes Week. One runs towards Egypt Point and the other lies approximately east/west, half way between the easterly beacon and the shore.

STANSWOOD BAY

To the east of Stansore Point, in Stanswood Bay, the shore is gently shelving and an echo sounder gives adequate guidance when working in to avoid a contrary tide. A west-going eddy may be found here close to the beach when the main stream is flooding strongly. If very close in near high water when taking advantage of the eddy one will need to watch out for the groynes. During World War II numerous sections of mulberry harbour were constructed at the top of the western beach, which accounts for its flat appearance. Further east there is a recommended water ski area off the Calshot shore to the west of Castle Point and Bourne Gap Buoys. There are also oyster beds in Stanswood Bay which are harvested periodically by a large number of fishing boats belonging to the 'Oyster Cooperative'. These boats will be towing twin dredges and may make unexpected manoeuvres. The dark-looking rectangular structure inshore of Bourne Gap Buoy, with tunnels leading to it, is the cooling water outlet from Fawley Power Station. It is lit and there are no particular obstructions surrounding it other than what can be seen. However there is some low profile junk around on the seabed, so it is not a good place to anchor. Further inshore there is an outfall marked by a red post. The pipe is 0.3m in diameter and rises about the same amount clear of the seabed in places.

There is public access to the Stanswood Bay beach between low and high water marks but severe erosion has affected the cliff face, and fallen trees are quite common.

CALSHOT

Many years ago Calshot used to be an island, distinguished by its Henry VIII fort. In present times the causeway beach is popular with windsurfers, water skiers, and dinghy sailors. The spit running south-eastwards from the causeway is an obvious trap for those unfamiliar with the Solent, as the spit extends deceptively far out from the shore, and also because some small craft can cross it at high water (*Plate 54*). One can work out routes for cutting the corner for a given draught and state of the tide, but if in doubt stay out, but not so far as to obstruct shipping in the main fairway. At low water one may need to take a course close to the Calshot side of the port hand channel navigation buoys to meet the conflicting requirements of sufficient depth of water and the need to leave the main fairway clear when a large ship is using it.

Plate 54. Calshot Spit looking north-eastwards.

Chapter 8
THE BRAMBLES TO HORSE SAND FORT

THE BRAMBLES

The Bramble Bank is shaped like an arrow-head pointing south-west. It is composed of blue clay covered by gravel and fine sand. Uffa Fox, and many others since, have played cricket on the bank at low water

Plate 55. The traditional game of cricket on the Brambles, pioneered by Uffa Fox. On this occasion my playful spaniel proved a deft fielder, but was reluctant to give the ball up in spite of pursuit by both batting and fielding teams.

spring tide (*Plate 55*) but the surface undulates somewhat which does not make for an entirely satisfactory pitch. West Knoll buoy and the Brambles post mark the Brambles adequately, but it is easy to misjudge the position of the bank or simply forget that it is there, and from time to time yachts are stranded on it for all to see. Unless the tide is high enough to pass over the Bramble Bank particular care is necessary to leave West Knoll to starboard when on a course from the west Solent towards Clipper Buoy. The Bramble Bank post is to the south-east of the bank and at most states of the tide yachts can safely

Plate 56. The Brambles, looking south towards Cowes. The post is to the left of the bank.

sail between the post and the bank (*Plate 56*).

East Knoll bank does not show up strongly on the chart and can be an embarrassment to larger yachts at low tide as can another large shallow area with a charted depth of less than one metre, extending one and a half miles to the east of the Bramble Bank. Being a relatively new arrival in the Solent this bank has no official name. Unofficially it is sometimes called the Limit Bank as it happens to lie at the limit of the Ports of Southampton and Portsmouth. At one low water in 1985 a British Admiral's Cup Team practice race had to be abandoned after most of the fleet had gone aground in this area.

Having invited due caution regarding the Bramble and adjoining banks, one should mention that the strength of the tide can be markedly weaker over these shallow areas. When there is sufficient depth to do so, this fact can be used to advantage when the tide is foul.

HILL HEAD TO BROWNDOWN POINT

Several old maps show Hillhead as Hell Head for some reason.

Historical records do mention that Titchfield Haven, also known as Hillhead Haven, was popular with smugglers. Also that in Nelsonian times sailors who could swim quite regularly deserted from His Majesty's warships and often ended up here on the beach. But all this hardly justifies such a severe description as Hell Head. Another point of historical interest is that the Meon River at one time allowed vessels to reach Titchfield from the sea. In the 17th Century a sea wall was constructed across the river mouth and a narrow canal was built for shipping, with lock gates at the seaward end. At the time this was not a popular decision with the local inhabitants as Titchfield depended upon sea trade for its prosperity. As had been expected the canal was not the success the river channel had been and use of the canal was discontinued altogether at the end of the 19th Century, but it can still be seen north of the coast road. The annual Tichfield carnival still celebrates the burning of an effigy of the third Earl of Southampton who was the owner of the land beside the Meon River and who was the perpetrator of the canal scheme. A final possible point of interest is that the Hill Head Sailing Club used to start their races from an old boatyard which operated from some shacks below the site of the present Osborne View Hotel. Much of the wood used to build the boatyard is said to have come from a pontoon which was commandeered after it

Plate 57. Exposed shingle banks and mudflats at the entrance of the Hamble River.

drifted over from the Royal Pier at Osborne Bay after a gale.

Nowadays the shallow Hill Head coastline should not be approached closely at low water (*Plate 57*) as it dries out some way from the shore. There are two particularly prominent banks. The first is the hard shell and shingle spit to the west of Hill Head Haven called Rainbow Bar. This is marked by a black and yellow post with a large yellow topmark shaped like a cross, often used as a drying out perch by cormorants (*Plate 58*). The other shingle spit, which has been growing for some years now, is adjacent to the water skiing area, marked by yellow buoys laid by the local council. It can also be located by knowing that it lies between the west end of the beach huts on the shore which are to be seen where the main road from Stubbington forks left for Lee-on-Solent, and right via Sea Lane towards Hillhead and a groyne to the west (*Plate 59*). The significance of this spit is that, in an area of gently shelving shingle, sand or mud there is a 100m long patch of prominent

Plate 58. The shingle and mud banks off Hillhead Harbour. The black and yellow post marking Rainbow Shoal is on the tip of the nearest promontory.

Plate 59. The rocky spit between Hillhead and Lee on Solent.

rocks dotted about off the spit, some of which dry at spring tides. Six hundred metres further east the concrete hovercraft slipway

Plate 60. The Lee on Solent hovercraft slipways, nowadays mainly used for launching sailing dinghies. There are yellow buoys on either side of the slipways.

at *HMS Daedalus* will be found, identifiable by the aircraft hangars behind. It extends some 100m into the Solent, but beyond this one can work the shingle beach closely as far as Lee Point (*Plate 60*), groynes, bathers, dinghies and canoes permitting. One could also mention that, with the prevailing wind as it is, the coastline between the Hamble and Gilkicker is exposed to the south-west and and should be treated with the respect due to any lee shore. Maybe this is how Lee on Solent acquired its name. At Lee Point there is a mud and sand spit extending 400m out (*Plate 61*). A green post marks the end of a surface water drain but the bank continues at least 50m beyond the post. At high water one can work the shore from Lee Point to Stokes Bay past the massive Browndown double sewer outfall marked by a green buoy. The square pipes are 1.8m in height but have been let into a trench with the intention of being deep enough to avoid even an aircraft carrier's anchor. Only the diffusers stick up from the seabed, and with a minimum depth of 11m they are not likely to present a hazard to yachtsmen. Though the sewer pipe may be disregarded, caution and

Plate 61. The mud and shingle bank off Lee Point looking north-west. The post is near the tip of the dark coloured Shingle bank.

close attention to the echo sounder is necessary along this shore at low water (*Plate* 62). The well-covered wreck 510m to the north-east of the Browndown buoy is the tank landing craft *LCT 1068*, which sank on 6th June 1947, complete with two tanks. Both the landing craft and

Plate 62. Looking south-east from Lee Point to Stokes Bay and Fort Gilkicker.

the tanks have sunk into the sand and can best be seen by divers after a south-easterly gale when the sand has been partially swept away. Other seabed objects nearby which have caught trawl nets or racing mark moorings are a steam pinnace 100m to the west of *LCT 1068* and an aircraft engine 620m west of Gilkicker Point. The pinnace was the patrol vessel for the old torpedo range which once existed off Browndown. That is until she was accidentally sunk by one of the trials torpedoes. The aircraft engine has twelve cylinders in line and is said to have come from a Dornier bomber.

STOKES BAY TO PORTSMOUTH HARBOUR
Stokes Bay is a popular haunt for bathers, wind surfers and fishermen, and so it may not be wise to go in close. At the west corner of Stokes

Bay a green post marks an exposed drain pipe, and also serves to indicate a growing ridge of gravel deposited by the adjacent surface water drain (*Plate 63*). In 1993 another green post was placed about half way along the bay - more or less opposite the Alverbank Hotel - where an

Plate 63. The gravel bank and exposed drain pipe at the west end of Stokes Bay, now marked by a green post rather than a buoy.

old drain pipe comes out above the beach level. In addition the bay has two notable obstructions. There is a dangerous wreck 520m offshore, opposite the Stokes Bay Sailing Club, of charted depth 0.9m, thought to be part of the lighter *Duddon* which sank in 1924. If one is working soundings up the shore, one should be north of a line between Gilkicker Point and Horse Sand Fort to be clear of this wreck. There are no plans to mark it. Apart from this, one can work the soundings all the way round the bay taking care to keep to seaward of a yellow conical buoy where the old pier used to be. This marks the other notable obstruction which is the remnants of the pier, still being removed by the Royal Engineers from Marchwood as a continuing training project. The current principal remnant is a crane tower in the form of a large inclined concrete block, sheathed in metal, showing one or two metres above the surface at low water (*Plate* 64). Other lumps of concrete protrude up to half a metre above the seabed. To avoid all these hazards when

Plate 64. The remains of the Stokes Bay Pier, marked by a yellow buoy.

making for the slipway just to the west of the yellow conical Pier Buoy, one needs to head for the red doors marked 'Gosport and Fareham Inshore Rescue' ensuring that one is to the west of a line extending from the lifeboat building's eastern wall, (i.e. if any of this wall is visible on the Gilkicker side, one is in danger of hitting one of the lumps of old pier). Both Stokes Bay slipways have a lip at their lower end which makes for serious difficulties with boat trailers at low water springs.

At high water Portsmouth an east-going eddy forms up to 150 metres from the shore at the east end of Stokes Bay and continues to run for the next two hours.

When close to Gilkicker Point one has to be careful of fishermen with rod and line, and the Mussel Patch shoal round the corner, once said to be good for lobsters. Just off Fort Monckton, the school for James Bonds, 600m north-east of Gilkicker, there is quite a collection of reinforced concrete blocks, reminiscent of invasion defences (*Plate 65*). They stand a metre above the seabed, and one or two of them are just exposed at extreme low springs. Once safely past these hazards,

Plate 65. Fort Monckton's collection of prominent reinforced concrete blocks are partially visible at low water spring tide.

the Inner Swashway channel can be used at high water as a short cut into Portsmouth Harbour. The Haslar wall has never been inviting as a landing place and is even less so now after recent salient reinforcements. Both this passage along the shore and Hamilton Bank are said to be building up with sand due to the cessation of nearby dredging operations.

Whatever channel is taken to Portsmouth Harbour entrance one should be wary of Hamilton Bank (*Plate 66*) which often dries out in the summer with the odd small craft on display. Even a battleship once sat out a tide there. A little further north, at the south-easterly corner of the west side of the Portsmouth Harbour entrance, a post marks the limit of the submerged structure of *HMS Dolphin* where a combination of adverse tide and a south-easterly wind seems to have brought about a number of groundings. On one occasion a catamaran even became wedged between the post and the sea wall.

Spit Sand is cut by the Swash Channel which ferries to the Isle of Wight use at high tide, but beware the numerous small obstructions between the outer and inner Swash Channels described on the chart, as they are solid blocks of up to 0.9m height. The unlit *Mary Rose* yellow wreck buoy is still in position about half a mile to the south of Spit Sand Fort as recovery operations continue. Other associated yellow unlit buoys may be found in the immediate vicinity, and one is asked to keep 300m clear.

Plate 66. Hamilton Bank awash, with a yacht stranded on its southern end. When a battleship went aground there many years ago, the officers of HMS Dolphin, the overlooking submarine base, jokingly offered the battleship officers honorary membership of their mess 'for the duration of their stay'.

THE FORTS

Spit Sand, Horse Sand and No Man's Land Forts might seem a bit too large and obvious to classify as hazards. Nevertheless in the past they were painted with black and white checks to make them more conspicuous to friendly shipping. They were built in the 1860s at vast expense to defend Portsmouth Dockyard against French invasion. It was originally intended that the inner fort should be on Sturbridge Shoal rather than Spit Sand but after fairly extensive work on the foundations it was discovered that the shoal was not solid enough. The same applied to a proposed fort on Ryde Sands. The designers wanted the sites so placed that ships in the channel would have to pass within 1000 yards of a fort, this being the range at which their guns could be sure to penetrate the heaviest armour used at that time. The protection and the armament of the forts themselves, particularly the two larger forts at Horse Sand and No Man's Land, is quite impressive, and it is clear that the defence of Portsmouth Harbour was taken seriously. For example the thickness of their stone lower walls was 18m, and the original plan was to have forty five 10-inch guns and forty four 12.5-inch guns in the casements with another ten 12-inch guns on the roof. As if that was not enough, a controlled minefield was also laid between the two larger forts.

As one would expect, the names of the forts are derived from the banks on which they were built. Ancient charts and maps show three large offshore banks in the area of the eastern entrance to the Solent called Horse Sand, No Man's Land and the Warner Shoal. It is not clear whether these banks ever dried out at low water, but it seems possible that they were a more distinct feature than they are today.

A fortuitous aid to self sufficiency is that they are all provided with good quality fresh water from 120m deep artesian wells. The forts were put up for sale in 1963 but no buyers came forward until the 1980s. Spit Sand Fort is now a museum, No Man's Land Fort was made an object of a stunningly expensive speculative development (see next chapter) and, finally, Horse Sand Fort was auctioned in October 1993, making £80,000.

HORSE SAND BARRIER

All that remains of the barrier between Horse Sand Fort and Southsea beach are the square concrete pedestals, with slightly variable heights, which become partially exposed at low water spring tides (*Plate 67*). These were built in about 1905 and would not be easy to remove. As intended, they are a menace, and trying to pass between them in a small craft towards low water without a chart or local knowledge is akin to Russian roulette. There is an account, for example, of the owner of a Nicholson 35 foot yacht coming to grief on her maiden voyage, after striking one of the pedestals when slipping away in the evening with his secret lady friend. The rescue services went into action and by the time the couple had dried out ashore, the media had ensured that their secret was no more. The owner of the yacht is reputed to have said that he took the same route with his previous boat on the way in to Portsmouth Harbour, and was most surprised to encounter the barrier on his way out.

The concrete pedestals are marked by a line of beacons and there is a charted inshore boat passage as well as the main passage half way between the fort and the Southsea shore.

Plate 67. Horse Sand Fort and the dangerous submerged barrier leading to Southsea beach. The main passage can be seen towards the top of the photograph and also a yacht approaching the southern end from the east. Her crew probably spotted the barrier as she tacked in the nick of time.

Chapter 9
NO MANS LAND FORT TO RYDE

NO MANS LAND BARRIER

Racing yachts are sometimes tempted to pass No Man's Land Fort very close on the north side and there have been reports of yachts grounding there at low water. This can be explained by the construction of both the No Man's Land and Horse Sand Fort walls which are vertical above sea level but take the form of annular Portland stone or granite steps underwater.

The submerged barrier, shown as extending 610m to the south west of No Man's Land Fort on the chart, has long been removed. There may be remains of the First World War or Second World War barriers still proud of the seabed, but the piles themselves, which on the Island side were driven into the seabed rather than held by concrete pedestals, have been entirely removed although not without difficulty. Nothing shows at an ordinary low water springs and no encounters have been heard of locally, but the Queen's Harbourmaster's surveyor at Portsmouth states that obstructions still exist which are occasionally visible at very low springs. Those who sail from Seaview have not seen any. Small vessels do now pass inshore of No Man's Land Fort at or near high water, and one can fairly safely assume that if there is a comfortable depth of water above chart datum for one's craft, then one can take the inshore passage.

Regarding the speculative development referred to above, a Chichester businessman sank a fortune into No Man's Land Fort when converting it into an unusual and exclusive fantasy home. There are enormous entertainment rooms, a revolving bed in the lighthouse suite, a tennis court, swimming pool, gymnasium, billiard room and three helipads, etc. All this, plus complete seclusion from the madding world and another 30,000 square feet of unconverted floor space, was originally on offer in 1990 for £5.75m. Only when the asking price came down to under £1m in 1993 was the fort, with all its lavish embellishments, eventually sold.

RYDE SANDS

A long thin spit, called the Debnigo, extends like a snake from the Island shore at Puckpool Point towards No Man's Land Fort (*Plate* 68). Inshore of this there is a 0.3m sewer pipe from Spring Vale which

Plate 68. *The Debnigo stretching out from Puckpool Point towards No Man's Land Fort.*

Plate 69. *Looking south-east from Ryde Pier over the whole expanse of Ryde Sands.*

usually shows well above the sea bed, this being dependent on the considerable sand movement of the Duver, the sandbank between Nettlestone and Spring Vale. The great expanse of Ryde Sands (*Plate 69*) is horseshoe shaped with the opening facing east. Some charts do not show this clearly and it is possible to work up the inside and become embayed. A new post has been placed to the north of the eastern tip of the outer spit of sand (*Plate 70*) and in working the soundings along the north side of the spit one should also watch out for the slightly more prominent sand banks which have formed on the

Plate 70. Looking east towards No Mans Land Fort. The outer spit of Ryde Sands can be seen in the foreground with the new post to the left of the tip.

corner opposite the South-West Mining Ground Buoy. It is possible to cross Ryde Sands at high water, and there is no danger from the new Ryde long sea outfall which goes from Appley right out to Sturbridge Shoal, and which is covered by at least 2m of sand. there used to be other pipes emerging from the shore to the west of the pier. Of these

74

the only hazardous one was the Ryde eastern outfall with its outer end marked with an unlit red beacon supported on scaffolding. This pipe and attendant marker structure has been entirely removed to allow freer access to the new Ryde Harbour which, incidentally, dries right out at low water.

As one might expect there is a prohibited anchorage area in the busy approaches to Ryde Pier. On the west side of the pier another outfall can be seen on the chart. This is a storm overflow pipe and has been recently renewed. Its seaward end is not marked as the pipe is entirely buried.

RYDE TO WOOTTON

There is not much tidal gradient to worry about over west Ryde Sands and yachts often find they do best on the edge of the shelf where there can be more wind. Binstead Rocks appear off the thickly wooded foreshore six cables to the west of the pier, making a natural harbour for small craft which can take the ground (*Plate 71*).

The west end of the rocks split the moorings, most of which are outside the rocks on the east side of the Binstead outfall.   The seaward half of this 0.6m pipe projects a good metre above the bottom with, incidentally, an older 0.22m disused pipe lying alongside it to the west. Therefore, if in doubt, one should go outside the red buoy marking the

Plate 71. Binstead Rocks, Binstead outfall and Binstead Hard,
looking south.

outer limit.   Binstead hard juts well out into the Solent beside the pipe but, with two posts to mark it, there is no identification problem by day. Binstead is one of several possible landing points along this shore, a private high water landing being found at the Tackling and Boating Club's pontoon opposite the moorings. Given permission, the pontoon is most convenient, and the hard will serve at low water.

When passing close to the shore one will find rocks on either side of Wootton Creek entrance (*Plate 72*).   The larger group are on the west side, and have a beacon sited in the middle which is helpful when passing offshore, or when using the high water short cut inshore of the rocks.   The red buoy marked on the chart to the north of Wootton Rocks is no longer laid.

Plate 72. Looking south-east towards Wootton Point. Rocks can be seen on either side of the creek. The most prominent are Wootton Rocks on the west side of the entrance.

Chapter 10
PEEL BANK TO COWES

KING'S QUAY CREEK

It is sometimes said that the name King's Quay Creek originated from a visit by King John who was seeking relaxation on the Isle of Wight after signing the Magna Carta. However the story seems unlikely as there was a civil war going on at this time and the Isle of Wight was not loyal to the king. King Charles I is also said to have landed there in 1647 after escaping from Hampton Court via Titchfield Haven, and this is the more likely explanation. It is an attractive and unspoilt drying inlet (*Plate 73*) but, except in a dinghy, difficult to enter even at high tide, and as the area is privately owned, no landing is allowed.

Plate 73. King's Quay Creek dries out completely at low water. Note the rocks off Barton Point, called East Patch, on the right hand side of the picture.

PEEL BANK

Half a mile north east of King's Quay Creek lies a red wreck buoy. The 'wreck' is a 16.5 x 5.4 x 2.7m reinforced concrete structure, probably a piece of mulberry harbour. It lies some 17m SSW of the buoy and might just show at extreme low water springs. One should note that the chart shows three patches on Peel Bank of less than 2m.

These, which include the obstruction 0.35 mile to the east of Peel Bank Buoy, are thought to be fragments of mulberry harbour too, as Peel Bank was the wartime mulberry anchorage. Apparently bits of steel rod stick out of them. There is a designated waterski area off King's Quay creek with the Peel Wreck Buoy at its centre, marked as 'buoyed' on the chart. However, unlike the water skiing area off Hillhead, no buoys are laid.

Plate 74. Osborne Bay, looking south. The bay dries out at low water spring tides and both vessels in this picture are aground.

OSBORNE BAY

Osborne Bay is shallow with many groynes, and reefs at each end (*Plate 74*). These are shown on charts off Barton Point but not at the western end of the bay where a drying patch of rocks appears about 150m offshore. Within the bay opposite the Tea House, as the large building on the beach with the central tower is known, the remnants of the Royal Hard extends over 400m out into the Solent.

NORRIS CASTLE TO THE SHRAPE MUD

Further west, racing yachts have been known to ground from time to time on the long finger of Norris Rocks (*Plate 75*). If working on soundings along the shore, Norris Buoy is too far offshore to be of help, but the west side of the gap in the woods marks them splendidly. As one passes the crumbling sea wall on the way towards Old Castle Point, the one time site of another Henry VIII castle, one should still keep an eye on the echo sounder as the sandy, boulder-strewn beach dries well out from the shore.   A contrary tide on the corner can drive the unwary inshore ready to fall victim to a small rocky ledge off Castle Point, not shown on the chart, or on to the Shrape Mud (*Plate 76*). This, at its seaward end, is a sand bank running about 200m north west from the Norris Castle summer house, the lone square building on the shore. The bank rises quite sharply from the sea bed and has tended to build in length and height over the last few years.

A large new sewer outfall was built off Old Castle Point in 1990 running 700m in a northerly direction from the point. The diffusers are beehive-shaped concrete constructions which could foul an anchor, but a decision was made not to mark them, as it is not a suitable anchoring place, and any more buoys in this area would only be confusing.

Plate 75. Looking south-east at the patch of rocks off Old Castle Point. Norris Rocks can be seen beyond, then the patch of rocks at the west end of Osborne Bay and the remnants of the pier towards the centre of Osborne Bay.

80

Plate 76. Looking south-east at the sand spit at the north end of the Shrape Mud. Local opinion has it that the spit is gradually growing in length towards the north-west.

INDEX

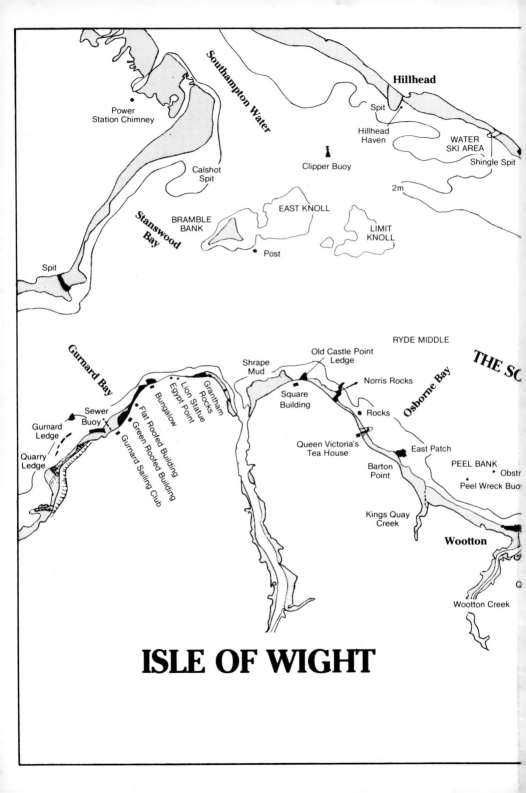

Southampton Water

Hillhead

Power Station Chimney

Spit

Hillhead Haven

WATER SKI AREA

Calshot Spit

Clipper Buoy

Shingle Spit

2m

Stanswood Bay

BRAMBLE BANK

EAST KNOLL

LIMIT KNOLL

Spit

Post

RYDE MIDDLE

Gurnard Bay

Shrape Mud

Old Castle Point Ledge

Norris Rocks

Osborne Bay

THE SO

Grantham Rocks

Lion Statue

Egypt Point

Square Building

Rocks

Sewer Buoy

Bungalow

Flat Roofed Building

Gurnard Ledge

Green Roofed Building

Quarry Ledge

Gurnard Sailing Club

Queen Victoria's Tea House

East Patch

PEEL BANK

Obstr

Peel Wreck Buo

Barton Point

Kings Quay Creek

Wootton

Wootton Creek

Q

ISLE OF WIGHT